THE GARLIC
COOKBOOK

THE GARLIC
COOKBOOK

THE ESSENCE OF THE
MEDITERRANEAN

BEVERLEY JOLLANDS

LORENZ BOOKS

This edition is published by Lorenz Books

Lorenz Books is an imprint of Anness Publishing Ltd
Hermes House, 88-89 Blackfriars Road, London SE1 8HA
tel. 020 7401 2077; fax 020 7633 9499
www.lorenzbooks.com; info@anness.com

© Anness Publishing Ltd 2003

This edition distributed in the UK by The Manning Partnership Ltd
6 The Old Dairy, Melcombe Road, Bath BA2 3LR
tel. 01225 478 444; fax 01225 478 440; sales@manning-partnership.co.uk

This edition distributed in the USA and Canada by National Book Network
4501 Forbes Boulevard, Suite 200, Lanham, MD20706;
tel. 301 459 3366; fax 301 429 5746; www.nbnbooks.com

This edition distributed in Australia by Pan Macmillan Australia
Level 18, St Martins Tower, 31 Market St, Sydney, NSW 2000
tel. 1300 135 113; fax 1300 135 103; customer.service@macmillan.com.au

This edition distributed in New Zealand by David Bateman Ltd
30 Tarndale Grove, Off Bush Road, Albany, Auckland
tel. (09) 415 7664; fax (09) 415 8892

Publisher: Joanna Lorenz
Managing Editor: Helen Sudell
Senior Editor: Joanne Rippin
Design: Nigel Partridge
Editorial Reader: Penelope Goodare
Production Controller: Darren Price

The Publishers would like to thank Bridgeman Art Library for permission to
reproduce the pictures on pages 8, 9, 12 and 13, and to Sylvia Cordaiy
Photo Library for the picture on page 11 (bottom right).

Recipes supplied by: Jacqueline Clark, Joanna Farrow, Brian Glover, Sally
Mansfield, Rena Salaman, Marlena Spieler, Kate Whiteman.

Recipe photography by: Eliza Baird, Martin Brigdale, Michelle Garrett,
William Lingwood.

10 9 8 7 6 5 4 3 2 1

Contents

INTRODUCTION 6

The History of Garlic 8

Growing and Types of Garlic 10

Garlic in Myth and Magic 12

The Healing Herb 14

COOKING WITH GARLIC 16

Garlic Techniques 18

Sauces, Relishes and Dips 20

Appetizers and Soups 26

Fish 36

Meat and Poultry 42

Vegetarian Dishes 50

Side Dishes 58

Index 64

Introduction

Garlic is a close relative of onions and leeks, and like both those vegetables, has been part of our diet for thousands of years – so long that no one really knows where it originated. Nowadays, it is grown all around the world, and its inimitable flavour is an important staple of many of the world's great cuisines. Today, when cooking styles are constantly evolving and fusing, the use of garlic is becoming more profuse and adventurous: cooks who once might just have nervously rubbed a single clove around a salad bowl now confidently toss it into pasta, mash it into potatoes or serve whole heads roasted with chicken or lamb.

Our growing love affair with garlic is spurred on by our increasing awareness of its therapeutic qualities. The old herbalists described it as a cure-all, and modern research is discovering that they were right to recommend it. It can fight infection, reduce blood pressure, lower cholesterol, and is being studied for possible protection against cancer.

Of course, the best reason to eat garlic is because it's delicious, and has a magical, transformative effect on a host of other foods. Whether it's raw and pungent or slow-cooked and mellow, garlic plays a starring role in all the recipes in this book.

The History of Garlic

Garlic (*Allium sativum*) is a member of the lily family. It grows wild in central Asia and is believed to have originated there, but the taste for it spread, and it is mentioned in 4,000-year-old Chinese texts. It is not difficult to grow, as long as it can have the long growing season it needs and a period of cold weather to initiate the development of the bulb, so cultivation was widespread. Over the centuries many different varieties have developed, most of them geographically specific because they have adapted to local climates and conditions.

The ancient Egyptians not only valued garlic as food, but gave it ceremonial significance and used it medicinally. As it was believed to be fortifying, it was

▼ Workmen constructing the great pyramids in ancient Egypt were strengthened by eating garlic.

▲ The ancient Greeks and Romans recognized garlic's healing properties and it was used to treat many conditions.

included in the rations of the workmen who built the Great Pyramid at Giza, and Herodotus found an inscription detailing the quantities they consumed. Ancient Greek and Roman medical texts prescribed it for a variety of conditions. Athletes ate it before competing, and soldiers before going into battle.

The stinking rose

As early as Roman times, upper-class Europeans considered it vulgar to eat garlic because of its smell, and this attitude lasted for many centuries. Cervantes' *Don Quixote*, published in the early 17th century, included the advice: "Do not eat garlic or onions; for their smell will reveal that you are a peasant". But while garlic was consigned to the diet of the rustic labourer, it was also still valued as a medicinal herb.

In medieval England it was given to fighting cocks to improve their chances, and recommended as a deterrent against moles in the garden. Nicholas Culpeper's *Herbal* of 1649 recommended it as a remedy for all diseases and hurts, from pains in the ears to bites from mad dogs. Garlic was a traditional defence against leprosy and tuberculosis, and garlands of it were worn to protect against the plague. It was the principal ingredient of "Four Thieves' Vinegar", which is supposed to have originated in Marseilles in 1722, when four thieves successfully used the mixture as protection against infection while they robbed the dead bodies of plague victims. Garlic garlands were even worn during the flu epidemic of 1918.

A new taste for garlic

In India and the Far East garlic was always a basic ingredient, and even Mrs Beeton acknowledged its merits in the chutneys and spicy sauces that found their way west during British rule in India. Around the Mediterranean it was central to traditional cuisine, giving classic recipes such as aioli and skorthalia their essential character. In our own age it has now become "chic to reek" in the English-speaking world; within a couple of generations, our increasingly cosmopolitan approach to food has turned garlic into a firm favourite in cultures that had previously shunned it, and it is now appreciated nearly everywhere.

Since the 1970s, enthusiasm for garlic has led to annual garlic festivals springing up all over the United States and Canada. The largest is held at Gilroy in California, where garlic devotees consume treats such as garlic sushi, garlic ice cream and garlic wine. There is also a British garlic festival on the Isle of Wight, where garlic thrives in the mild climate.

▼ For centuries, European aristocrats regarded garlic as smelly food fit only for peasants – who wisely ignored them.

Growing and Types of Garlic

The word garlic is Anglo-Saxon, derived from *gar*, a spear, and *leac*, a plant, and refers to the shape of the growing leaves. A perennial, it grows to about 60cm/2ft, with upright leaves and a single tall flower stem. Bulbs are generally harvested in the autumn and dried off in the sun before being stored.

The bulb or head is composed of separate cloves, each wrapped in its own skin, and the whole head is enclosed in a further layer of skin, which becomes papery as it matures. Garlic can be stored for months in cool, dry, airy conditions, and is often tied up and sold in strings. New-season or "fresh" garlic, sold in early summer before the skin has dried, is creamy white, flushed with green and pink.

▼ Heads of garlic are braided in strings and hung up to dry before being transported to markets and stores.

▲ Prettily coloured, new season's garlic has a deliciously mild flavour and is a special treat in the summer.

Garlic bulbs vary widely in size. The tiniest varieties are those grown in South-east Asia, which have only four to six cloves in each bulb. In general, larger cloves have a milder and less pungent flavour. The colour of the skin also varies, from white, such as the Californian Silverskin, through pink to purple.

Cultivation

Garlic needs a sunny situation in moist, free-draining soil. To grow successfully, it needs a period of cold, and it can be planted throughout the autumn until early winter. Although it is possible to grow garlic from cloves bought for cooking, you will get better results from specially produced bulbs. Plant the cloves at about twice their own depth and 10cm/4in apart, leaving 30cm/12in between the rows. Keep the rows free of weeds, and lift the plants as soon as the leaves start to fade.

The first green shoots that appear in early spring are considered a delicacy in southern France, Spain and Italy, where they are used in much the same way as chives or spring onions (scallions). They are also popular in Chinese stir-fries.

Wild garlic and other relatives

Although *Allium sativum* now grows wild only in central Asia, some native alliums of other regions are locally known as wild garlic. *A. canadense*, also known as meadow leek, is found in North America. It has a mild flavour and can be cooked like leeks. Elephant garlic, *A. ampeloprasum*, is more closely related to leeks than to garlic. It comes from the Levant but is now cultivated in the United States, producing heads weighing up to 450g/1lb.

European wild garlics include field garlic (*A. vineale*). The bulb is extremely pungent, but the young spring shoots are used in salads. In Britain, wild garlic is usually *A. ursinum* or ramsons, a beautiful woodland plant with starry white spring flowers and a strong garlic smell. Its young leaves can be added to a wide variety of dishes.

Smoked garlic

Whole heads of garlic are sometimes hot-smoked so that they are partly cooked and infused with the aroma of wood smoke. The peeled, crushed cloves can be used to make garlic butter or mayonnaise.

▼ *Allium sativum* is relatively easy to grow and should be a feature of every worthwhile kitchen garden.

▼ If using wild garlic leaves, pick them before the plant flowers and use them in salads, sauces, soups and cheese dishes.

Garlic in Myth and Magic

The curative qualities of garlic are well documented, and it is perhaps for this reason that many cultures have used it to ward off evil. Braids of garlic were once believed to protect the home from thieves and repel envious people – as well as, most famously, guarding against vampires. The ancient Greeks placed garlic at crossroads to placate Hecate, the goddess of the Underworld, and this practice continued well into the 11th century AD, when the Church put a stop to it. Another curious superstition is the idea, recounted by many classical authors, that garlic could rob magnets of their power.

According to one legend, garlic was not found growing in the Garden of Eden – perhaps because of its rank smell. A Muslim myth tells that it arose after the Fall: as Satan victoriously left the Garden, garlic grew on the spot where he placed his left foot, and onion from his right footprint. An Indian legend tells of the god Vishnu decapitating King Rahu, lord of the demons, as a punishment for stealing the elixir of life. Garlic is said to have sprung from where his blood fell.

The protective herb

Garlic's protective powers have often been used at night. A clove would be put under the pillows of sleeping children to protect them, and dreaming about garlic was a sign of good luck to come, while

▲ Throughout the world, the mere presence of garlic has been regarded as a protection against and a cure for many diseases.

dreaming of eating garlic meant that a secret would be discovered. An Irish folk belief is that garlic planted on a Good Friday will protect people from fever throughout the entire year.

From Mexico to China, garlic has been considered to give protection from the evil eye, witches and demons. Sailors have carried it to protect them from shipwreck, and brides kept a clove in their pocket to keep evil away and bring good luck. In the American West, a girl who wanted to be rid of an unwanted lover had to leave a garlic clove with two crossed pins at a crossroads. If she could entice the man concerned to walk over it, he would lose interest in her.

In some parts of Europe, runners still chew garlic before a race to stop anyone getting ahead of them, and in Hungary it is fastened to the bit of a racehorse. Spanish bullfighters wear a clove as an amulet to protect them from being gored.

Garlic, vampires and witches

Just as a garland of garlic had been worn in medieval times as protection from the plague, it was also the traditional form of protection against vampires. When Bram Stoker used this motif in *Dracula* in 1897, he was recording a custom that had persisted for centuries in Slavic countries. An aversion to garlic was taken as a sign of vampirism, and garlic was even distributed in churches to make sure that their congregations were entirely human.

Garlands of garlic were hung around doorways to ward off visits from vampires and witches, and the recommended method of destroying the vampire (after driving a stake through its heart) was to decapitate the body and stuff its mouth with garlic. For fear of vampires emerging from their graves, the coffins of the dead were once strewn with garlic to keep the corpses inside. One modern explanation of the vampire myth is that it was inspired by porphyria, a liver disease whose symptoms include sensitivity to sunlight – and to garlic.

▲ Garlic has a long tradition of association with the diabolical – sometimes on the side of good, at other times on the side of evil. One of its positive uses was to drive away witches.

The Healing Herb

Garlic features in Ayurvedic and traditional Chinese medicine, as well as in the Western tradition, and some modern scientific studies support the idea that eating raw garlic regularly is beneficial. It is also valuable in a number of ways when used externally. The main active constituent is a sulphur compound called allicin, which is released only when the clove is crushed or bruised, and is destroyed by heat. So to be effective as a remedy, garlic needs to be eaten raw.

Medicinal uses of garlic

Regular consumption of garlic has been shown to reduce blood pressure and reduce the risk of blood clots. (Because it thins the blood, anyone taking anti-clotting drugs should seek medical advice before taking garlic therapeutically.) Garlic lowers blood cholesterol levels, while raising the level of beneficial

▲ Garlic contains over 30 therapeutic compounds. Allicin is destroyed by cooking, but most of the others remain active.

cholesterol, HDL. It has also been found to stimulate cell growth, and may guard against some kinds of cancer – the Chinese have taken it for centuries to protect against bowel cancer.

Garlic is a natural antibiotic, with the advantage that it does not destroy the beneficial bacteria in the intestine. It relieves catarrh and sinusitis, and wards

◄ Garlic capsules, or "pearls", provide all the benefits of eating raw garlic, but without making the breath smell unpleasant.

off cold germs. It deters or kills various parasites such as intestinal worms (if you can persuade cats and dogs to eat garlic, it will guard them against infestations of fleas and worms).

Cold cure

Taking raw garlic regularly should protect you from colds, but if you are already suffering from one, this traditional cure can help to relieve the symptoms:

15ml/1 tbsp clear honey
juice of 1 lemon
3–4 slices of fresh root ginger
pinch of cayenne pepper
2 cloves garlic, crushed

Put all the ingredients in a heatproof jug (pitcher) and pour on 250ml/8fl oz/1 cup boiling water. Leave to infuse (steep) for 10 minutes, then strain, reheat until warm and drink immediately.

External treatments

Garlic was used as an antiseptic wound dressing during World War I, and it combats various skin problems and infections. It is also antifungal, so can be used to treat conditions such as thrush or athlete's foot – for example, as a mixture of fresh garlic juice and live yogurt. Warm garlic oil, made by macerating crushed garlic in olive oil, is a traditional treatment for earache, especially in babies and children.

The smell

To remove the smell of garlic from your hands and fingers, sprinkle them with salt and rinse in cold water before washing with hot water and soap. Another way is to rub over your hands with a piece of lemon before washing in hot water. Lemon can also be used to freshen chopping boards that have been used to prepare garlic.

To counteract the smell of garlic on the breath, chew fresh parsley, caraway seeds or a cinnamon stick, or suck a coffee bean.

▼ A syrup made from garlic, honey and ginger is a traditional cure for colds and soothes sore throats.

Cooking with Garlic

Garlic has been used in cooking for centuries,
for both its inimitable flavour and its medicinal
properties. Garlic is added to sauces and dressings,
tucked into roasts, used to flavour casseroles, baked
with fish, beaten into mashed potato and used to
garnish savoury dishes of every kind. It may simply
enhance the flavours of other ingredients or take a
starring role, especially in soups and vegetable
dishes. The ways it is used range from the most
delicate hint in flavoured oils to serving
whole heads with a dish. There is no end to its
versatility. When raw, it has a powerful pungent
flavour, in braised dishes it is more subtle and
delicate, while roasting makes it taste wonderfully
rich and mellow. It features in dishes from all over
the world from spicy Thai curries to Mediterranean
fish stews and from North African relishes to Indian
dhals. The following recipes demonstrate the
fabulous scope and versatility of this small
but essential ingredient.

Garlic Techniques

Eaten raw, garlic has a very strong flavour, but when gently roasted it loses its pungency and becomes sweet, mellow, creamy and delicious. Most cultures consider garlic as a herb or flavouring, rather than a vegetable in its own right, although some dishes call for several whole heads of garlic, such as the classic French recipe for chicken with forty cloves of garlic, Spanish garlic soup, or southern Indian dishes of whole garlic cloves cooked with spices and coconut milk. Crisp fried garlic is a popular garnish in Burma, and pickled garlic is eaten as an accompaniment to many Thai and Korean dishes.

Peeling

For most purposes, garlic cloves need to be peeled before cooking. Simply cut off the base of the clove and peel off the skin with your fingers. Alternatively, place the clove on a board, lay the flat of a knife blade over it and press down sharply with the heel of your hand. You can also buy a special garlic peeler, which consists of a small rubber tube. The cloves go inside this and you then roll it back and forth on a flat surface to loosen the skin.

Crushing and chopping

This produces the strongest, most pungent flavour. Peel the cloves and crush them with a mortar and pestle, or crush them on a chopping board with the

▲ When you close the handles of a garlic press, the flat face pushes the garlic through the holes in the base.

flat blade of a knife. Adding a little salt will make this much easier. Alternatively, use a garlic press: to avoid the metal press tainting the flavour of the garlic pulp (and to make the press easier to clean) do not peel the clove before crushing it. If you want a milder flavour, chop or slice the garlic.

Blanching

Plunge the cloves into boiling water for 2–3 minutes to reduce their pungency. If you are peeling a large amount of garlic, this also makes the job easier as the cloves will simply slip out of their skins.

Frying

Many recipes begin by softening chopped or crushed garlic in oil, usually with onions. It's important not to allow the garlic to brown, as it will taste bitter.

Garlic-flavoured oil

Lightly crush a peeled clove and cook gently in the oil required by the recipe until lightly coloured, then remove it before adding any other ingredients.

Preserved garlic

In many countries, garlic is pickled in vinegar or preserved in oil, for adding to salads, egg and rice dishes. You can do this yourself, or buy bottles of pickled garlic in Asian supermarkets. Ready-made garlic purées (pastes) are available, but preservatives tend to alter the flavour.

Roasted garlic purée

This useful flavouring will keep for several weeks if the surface of the purée is covered with oil to a depth of at least 1cm/½ in. It is good in soufflés, omelettes and tarts, or simply spread on good bread and eaten with grilled (broiled) or baked goat's cheese. To make a simple pasta sauce, stir 30–45ml/2–3 tbsp of the purée into 150ml/¼ pint/⅔ cup double (heavy) cream, heated until it is bubbling. Season and add a squeeze of lemon and some chopped basil.

5 large heads of garlic
2–3 fresh thyme or rosemary sprigs, or both
extra virgin olive oil
salt and ground black pepper

Makes about 120ml/4fl oz/½ cup

1 Preheat the oven to 190°C/375°F/Gas 5. Cut a thin slice off the top of each garlic head, and wrap the heads in foil with the herbs and 45ml/3 tbsp oil. Bake for 50–60 minutes until very soft, then cool.

2 Gently squeeze the garlic out of its skin into a bowl and mash with a little more extra virgin olive oil and seasoning. Spoon into a sterilized jar and cover with a 1cm/½ in layer of oil.

◀ Garlic cloves may be preserved in oil or pickled in vinegar and are widely available from Asian food stores.

SAUCES, RELISHES AND DIPS

Raw or roasted garlic, crushed to a creamy purée, enlivens numerous classic dips and sauces for pasta, meat and vegetables. If you find raw garlic too pungent, tone it down by blanching the cloves in boiling water before crushing them.

Garlic and Pepper Dressing

This dressing is delicious on salads of chicken or chargrilled vegetables or stirred into hot or cold pasta.

Serves 4

2 large heads of garlic
3 fresh thyme sprigs
150ml/¼ pint/⅔ cup olive oil
2 red (bell) peppers, halved and seeded
juice of ½ lemon
15ml/1 tbsp chopped fresh chives
salt and ground black pepper

1 Preheat the oven to 190°C/375°F/ Gas 5. Wrap the garlic in foil with the thyme and 15ml/1 tbsp oil and bake for 35–45 minutes, until soft. At the same time, place the red peppers, cut sides down, on a baking sheet, and bake until their skins are blistered.

2 Cover the peppers with a clean dishtowel for 10 minutes, then remove the skins and place the flesh in a food processor or blender. Add the garlic pulp by squeezing it out of the skins, and pour in any cooking juices from the foil. Process the mixture until smooth.

3 With the motor running, slowly blend in the remaining olive oil, then the lemon juice through the feeder tube. Season to taste with salt and pepper and stir in the chopped fresh chives.

Thai Green Curry Paste

Makes about 120ml/4fl oz/½ cup

3 Thai shallots, chopped
3–4 garlic cloves, chopped
4 fresh green chillies, seeded
and chopped
2 lemon grass stalks, outer leaves
removed, chopped
2.5cm/1in piece fresh galangal or fresh
root ginger, chopped
15g/½oz/½ cup fresh coriander
(cilantro) leaves and root, chopped
2 kaffir lime leaves
5ml/1 tsp ground roasted
coriander seeds
2.5ml/½ tsp ground roasted cumin
15–25ml/3–5 tsp Thai fish sauce
15–30ml/1–2 tbsp groundnut
(peanut) oil
pinch of light muscovado (brown) sugar
salt and ground black pepper

This popular sauce is authentically quite hot, but you can reduce the number of chillies for a milder version.

1 Put the shallots, garlic, chillies, lemon grass, galangal or ginger, fresh coriander, lime leaves, ground coriander and ground cumin in a food processor or blender.

2 Add fish sauce to taste and process briefly. Pour in sufficient groundnut oil to make a paste. Season with salt, pepper and sugar.

Walnut and Garlic Sauce

Serves 4

2 × 1cm/½ in slices white bread,
crusts removed
60ml/4 tbsp milk
150g/5oz/1¼ cups shelled walnuts
4 garlic cloves, chopped
120ml/4fl oz/½ cup olive oil
15–30ml/1–2 tbsp walnut oil, plus extra
for drizzling
juice of 1 lemon
salt and ground black pepper
paprika, for dusting

This flavoursome sauce comes from the Mediterranean region, where several versions are found. Serve it with roast chicken or with steamed cauliflower or potatoes. It is also traditionally served with salt cod.

1 Place the bread in a shallow dish, pour over the milk and leave to soak for about 5 minutes. Transfer the bread to a food processor or blender, add the walnuts and garlic and process to a coarse paste. With the motor running, gradually add the olive oil and walnut oil through the feeder tube to make a smooth, thick sauce.

2 Stir in lemon juice to taste and season with salt and pepper. Transfer the sauce to a small serving bowl, drizzle with a little extra walnut oil and dust the surface lightly with paprika.

Mushroom, Garlic and Red Onion Preserve

Makes about 600ml/1 pint/2½ cups

500g/1¼lb mixed mushrooms, such as
ceps, chestnut mushrooms, shiitake
and girolles
300ml/½ pint/1¼ cups white
wine vinegar
15ml/1 tbsp sea salt
5ml/1 tsp sugar
300ml/½ pint/1¼ cups water
4–5 fresh bay leaves
8 large fresh thyme sprigs
15 garlic cloves, halved
1 small red onion, thinly sliced
2–3 small dried red chillies
5ml/1 tsp coriander seeds
5ml/1 tsp black peppercorns
few strips of lemon rind
250–350ml/8–12fl oz/1–1½ cups
olive oil

Garlicky pickled mushrooms make a delicious addition to mixed antipasti.

1 Trim and wipe the mushrooms and cut the large ones in half. Put the vinegar, salt, sugar and water in a pan and bring to the boil. Add the herbs, garlic, sliced onion, spices and lemon rind and simmer for 2 minutes.

2 Add the mushrooms and simmer for 3–4 minutes, then drain, retaining the herbs and spices. Place the mushrooms, herbs and spices in a sterilized jar and pour in enough olive oil to cover by at least 1cm/½in.

3 Leave the preserve to settle, then tap the jar to dispel any air bubbles. Seal and leave for at least 2 weeks in a cool, dark place before using.

Cacik

This light, garlicky yogurt dip is served all around the eastern Mediterranean with olives and bread, and is also used to accompany meat dishes.

Serves 6

1 small cucumber
300ml/½ pint/1¼ cups thick natural (plain) yogurt
3 garlic cloves, crushed
30ml/2 tbsp chopped fresh mint
30ml/2 tbsp chopped fresh dill or parsley
salt and ground black pepper
fresh mint and dill or parsley sprigs, to garnish
olive oil, olives and pitta bread, to serve

1 Finely chop the cucumber and layer in a colander with plenty of salt. Leave to drain for 30 minutes, then rinse thoroughly under cold running water and drain. Pat thoroughly dry on kitchen paper.

2 Mix together the yogurt, garlic and herbs in a serving bowl and season to taste with salt and pepper. Stir in the cucumber. Garnish with herbs, drizzle with a little olive oil, and serve with olives and freshly-warmed rounds of pitta bread.

Garlic Mayonnaise

Serves 4–6

2 large (US extra large) egg yolks
pinch of dry mustard
up to 300ml/½ pint/1¼ cups mild
olive oil
15–30ml/1–2 tbsp lemon juice or white
wine vinegar
2–4 garlic cloves
salt and ground black pepper

You can vary the flavour of this lovely dressing by using roasted garlic purée or puréed smoked garlic instead of raw garlic. Serve it as a dip with crunchy raw vegetables, or with fried potatoes, chicken or fish.

1 Whisk the egg yolks with the mustard and a pinch of salt in a bowl. Whisk in the oil, one drop at a time to begin with. Once the mixture starts to thicken, pour the oil in a steady stream.

2 Stop adding the oil when the mayonnaise is as thick as soft butter. Add lemon juice or vinegar to taste, and season with salt and pepper. Crush the garlic to a pulp and stir it in until well combined.

APPETIZERS AND SOUPS

Garlic-flavoured dishes make a great start to any meal as they really wake up the taste buds.
Serve the tempting treats that follow with plenty of crusty bread, fresh rolls or with the fragrant
garlic and herb bread described below.

Garlic and Herb Bread

Serves 6

115g/4oz/½ cup unsalted (sweet)
butter, softened

5–6 large garlic cloves, finely chopped
or crushed

45ml/3 tbsp chopped fresh herbs

1 baguette or bloomer loaf

salt and ground black pepper

*Excellent with soups or vegetables, garlic bread is also irresistible on its
own. For a change, you could also try flavouring the butter with a mixture
of garlic, chopped chilli, grated lime rind and chopped coriander (cilantro).*

1 Preheat the oven to 200°C/400°F/Gas 6. Beat the butter with the garlic,
chopped herbs and seasoning.

2 Using a serrated knife, cut the loaf into 1cm/½in thick diagonal slices,
leaving them still attached at the base. Spread the butter evenly between the
slices, and spread any remaining butter
over the top of the loaf.

3 Wrap the loaf in foil to enclose it
completely and bake for about
20–25 minutes, until the butter is
melted and the crust is crisp.

4 Unwrap the loaf and separate the
slices to serve. You can usually just pull
them apart with your fingers, but be
careful as the butter will be hot.

Florentine Garlic Artichokes

This refreshing garlic-flavoured artichoke appetizer is perfect for serving on a summer's day when fresh artichokes are in abundance.

1 To prepare the artichokes, remove the tough leaves, peel the tender part of the stems and cut into bitesize pieces. Quarter the artichokes and remove the inedible hairy chokes.

2 Heat the oil in a large pan and cook the onion and garlic for 5 minutes, until softened. Stir in the parsley and cook for a few seconds, then add the wine, stock and artichokes. Season with half the lemon juice, salt and pepper.

3 Simmer for 15 minutes, until the artichokes are tender, then lift them out with a slotted spoon and transfer to a serving dish. Increase the heat and reduce the cooking liquid by about half. Pour over the artichokes and add the remaining lemon juice. Leave to cool before serving.

Serves 4

4 globe artichokes
60ml/4 tbsp olive oil
1 onion, chopped
5–8 garlic cloves, coarsely chopped or thinly sliced
30ml/2 tbsp chopped fresh parsley
120ml/4fl oz/½ cup dry white wine
120ml/4fl oz/½ cup vegetable stock or water
juice of 1–2 lemons
salt and ground black pepper

Roasted Garlic with Goat's Cheese, Walnut and Herb Pâté

Serves 4

4 large heads of garlic
4 fresh rosemary sprigs
8 fresh thyme sprigs
60ml/4 tbsp olive oil
salt and ground black pepper

For the pâté:
200g/7oz soft goat's cheese
5ml/1 tsp finely chopped fresh thyme
15ml/1 tbsp chopped fresh parsley
50g/2oz/½ cup shelled
walnuts, chopped
15ml/1 tbsp walnut oil
fresh thyme and shelled walnuts,
to garnish

To serve:
4–8 slices sourdough bread

The combination of sweet, mellow roasted garlic and smooth, tangy goat's cheese is a classic one. This pâté is particularly good when it is made with fresh, new season's walnuts.

1 Preheat the oven to 190°C/375°F/Gas 5. Strip the papery skin from the garlic heads. Place them in an ovenproof dish into which they fit snugly. Tuck the rosemary and thyme around the garlic.

2 Drizzle the garlic with the oil and season with salt and black pepper. Cover closely with foil and bake for 35 minutes, basting once. Leave to cool.

3 Preheat the grill (broiler). To make the pâté, cream the cheese with the thyme, parsley and chopped walnuts. Beat in 15ml/1 tbsp of the cooking oil from the garlic and season to taste. Transfer to a serving bowl.

4 Brush the slices of sourdough bread with the remaining cooking oil from the garlic, and toast under the grill.

5 Drizzle the walnut oil over the pâté, and grind some black pepper over it. Place a garlic head on each plate and serve with the pâté and slices of toast. Garnish with a little fresh thyme and a few shelled walnuts.

Roasted Beetroot with Skorthalia

Serves 4

675g/1½ lb medium or small
beetroot (beets)
75–90ml/5–6 tbsp olive oil
salt

For the skorthalia:
4 medium slices of white bread, crusts
removed, soaked in water for
10 minutes
2–3 garlic cloves, chopped
15ml/1 tbsp white wine vinegar
60ml/4 tbsp olive oil

This frugal but flavoursome garlic sauce was eaten by the ancient Greeks, and is still a favourite all around the eastern Mediterranean. Beetroot is a popular winter vegetable in Greece, but the sauce is also excellent with other vegetables and with fried fish.

1 Preheat the oven to 180°C/350°F/Gas 4. Rinse the beetroot, being careful not to pierce the skin. Place in a roasting pan lined with a large sheet of foil, drizzle with a little of the olive oil and season with salt. Fold over the foil to enclose the beetroot and bake for about 1½ hours, until soft.

2 To make the sauce, squeeze most of the water out of the bread and place it in a food processor or blender with the garlic and vinegar. Process until smooth, then, with the motor running, drizzle in the olive oil through the feeder tube. Spoon into a serving bowl.

3 When the beetroot are cool enough to handle, peel and slice them and arrange in a flat dish or on individual plates. Drizzle the remaining olive oil over them and serve with the skorthalia.

Potato Skorthalia
Use only 2 soaked slices of bread and process them with 1 large cooked potato that has been coarsely mashed before adding the garlic and vinegar and processing again.

Parsnips and Chickpeas with Spicy Garlic Paste

Serves 4

200g/7oz dried chickpeas, soaked
overnight in cold water, then drained
7 garlic cloves, finely chopped
1 small onion, finely chopped
5cm/2in piece of fresh root
ginger, chopped
2 fresh green chillies, seeded and
finely chopped
60ml/4 tbsp groundnut (peanut) oil
5ml/1 tsp cumin seeds
10ml/2 tsp ground coriander seeds
5ml/1 tsp ground turmeric
5ml/1 tsp chilli powder or mild paprika
50g/2oz/½ cup cashew nuts, toasted
and ground
250g/9oz tomatoes, peeled and chopped
900g/2lb parsnips, cut into chunks
5ml/1 tsp ground roasted cumin
juice of 1 lime, to taste
salt and ground black pepper
fresh coriander (cilantro) leaves and a
few toasted cashew nuts, to garnish

In this Indian-style dish, the sweet flavour of parsnips is beautifully balanced by a spicy paste of garlic, onion, chilli and ginger. Serve it with Indian breads to mop up the sauce.

1 Put the soaked chickpeas in a pan, add sufficient cold water to cover and bring to the boil. Boil vigorously for 10 minutes, then reduce the heat and simmer for 1–1½ hours, until tender. Drain well.

2 Reserving 10ml/2 tsp garlic, put the rest in a food processor or blender with the onion, ginger and half the chillies. Add 75ml/5 tbsp water and process to a smooth paste.

3 Heat the oil in a large frying pan and cook the cumin seeds over a low heat for 30 seconds, until they give off their aroma. Stir in the coriander seeds, turmeric, chilli powder or paprika and ground cashew nuts. Add the blended paste and cook, stirring, until the liquid has evaporated.

4 Stir in the tomatoes and cook for 5 minutes, then add the chickpeas and parsnips with 450ml/¾ pint/scant 2 cups water. Season to taste with salt and pepper, bring to the boil and simmer, uncovered, for 15–20 minutes, until the parsnips are tender and the sauce is thick.

5 Add the ground roasted cumin and season with salt and lime juice to taste. Stir in the reserved garlic and chilli and cook for a further 1–2 minutes. Transfer to a warmed dish and serve immediately, sprinkled with coriander leaves and toasted cashew nuts.

Chilled Garlic and Almond Soup

Serves 6

75g/3oz/¾ cup blanched almonds
50g/2oz/½ cup pine nuts
6 large garlic cloves, peeled
200g/7oz white bread, crusts removed,
soaked in water for 10 minutes
120ml/4fl oz/½ cup olive oil, plus extra
to serve
15ml/1 tbsp sherry vinegar
1 litre/1¾ pints/4 cups still mineral
water or filtered water, chilled
30–45ml/2–3 tbsp dry sherry
250g/9oz grapes, peeled, halved
and seeded
salt and ground white pepper
ice cubes and chopped fresh chives,
to garnish

Almonds and pine nuts are typical ingredients in southern Spain, and this creamy summer soup is based on an ancient Moorish recipe.

1 Roast the almonds and pine nuts together in a dry pan over medium heat until lightly browned. Cool and grind finely. Blanch the garlic in boiling water for 3 minutes, then drain.

2 Squeeze the bread and place in a food processor or blender with the garlic, nuts and 5ml/1 tsp salt. Process to a smooth paste, then gradually blend in the oil, vinegar and enough mineral water to make a creamy consistency.

3 Stir in the sherry to taste. Chill for at least 3 hours, then adjust the seasoning and add more water if necessary. Stir most of the grapes into the soup. Serve garnished with ice cubes, the remaining grapes and fresh chives.

Potato and Garlic Broth

Serves 4

Although there is plenty of garlic in this soup, it is roasted to give a sweet, mellow flavour. Served piping hot, it makes a perfect winter warmer.

2 large heads of garlic (about 20 cloves)
4 medium potatoes, diced
1.75 litres/3 pints/7½ cups vegetable stock
salt and ground black pepper
fresh flat leaf parsley, to garnish

1 Preheat the oven to 190°C/375°F/Gas 5. Strip the papery skin from the garlic heads and place them in an ovenproof dish into which they fit snugly. Cover closely with foil and bake for 35–45 minutes, until tender.

2 Meanwhile, par-boil the potatoes in lightly salted water for 10 minutes. Simmer the stock for 5 minutes, then add the drained potatoes.

3 Squeeze the garlic pulp into the soup, reserving a few cloves. Stir and season to taste with salt and pepper. Simmer for 15 minutes and serve garnished with the reserved garlic and parsley.

FISH

Buttery, garlic-laden sauces make an irresistible accompaniment to robustly flavoured roasted or grilled fish and, of course, garlic is an essential ingredient of the hearty fish soups and stews for which the Mediterranean is so justly famous.

Fish Soup with Rouille

Serves 6

1kg/2¼lb mixed fish
75ml/5 tbsp olive oil
1 each onion, carrot and leek, chopped
2 large ripe tomatoes, chopped
1 red (bell) pepper, seeded and chopped
2 garlic cloves, peeled and left whole
150g/5oz/⅔ cup tomato purée (paste)
1 fresh bouquet garni
300ml/½ pint/1¼ cups dry white wine
2 garlic cloves, coarsely chopped
5ml/1 tsp coarse salt
1 fresh red chilli, seeded and chopped
1 thick slice of white bread, crust removed, soaked in water and squeezed
salt, ground black pepper and cayenne pepper
6 slices baguette, toasted
100g/4oz Gruyère cheese, grated

This wonderfully flavoursome soup is traditionally served topped with toasted slices of baguette sprinkled with finely grated Gruyère cheese.

1 Cut the fish into large chunks, removing any obvious bones. Heat 300ml/2 tbsp of the oil in a large pan and cook the fish and chopped vegetables, stirring constantly, until they begin to colour.

2 Add the whole garlic, tomato purée, bouquet garni and wine, with just enough cold water to cover. Season with salt and pepper, bring to the boil, cover and simmer gently for 1 hour.

3 Meanwhile, to make the rouille, place the chopped garlic, coarse salt and chilli in a food processor or blender with the soaked bread and process to a smooth paste. Gradually blend in the remaining olive oil to make a smooth, shiny sauce. Season to taste with salt and cayenne.

4 When the soup is cooked, discard the bouquet garni and process the soup, in batches, in a food processor or blender, then pass through a sieve into a clean pan. Reheat the soup without allowing it to boil. Check the seasoning. Serve in individual bowls topped with slices of toasted baguette, grated Gruyère and a spoonful of rouille.

Provençal Aioli with Salt Cod

Serves 6

1kg/2¼lb salt cod, soaked overnight in
water and drained
1 fresh bouquet garni
18 small new potatoes, scrubbed
1 large fresh mint sprig
225g/8oz green beans, trimmed
225g/8oz broccoli florets
6 hard-boiled eggs
12 baby carrots, scrubbed
1 large red (bell) pepper, seeded and cut
into strips
2 fennel bulbs, cut into strips
18 cherry tomatoes
6 large whole cooked prawns (shrimp),
to garnish

For the aioli:
3–5 garlic cloves
2 large (US extra large) egg yolks
300ml/½ pint/1¼ cups olive oil
15–30ml/1–2 tbsp lemon juice or white
wine vinegar
salt and ground black pepper

This substantial and colourful salad, with garlic mayonnaise, constitutes a meal on its own and is perfect for summer entertaining.

1 Place the cod in a shallow pan and add water to cover and the bouquet garni. Bring to a simmer and poach for 10 minutes, until it flakes easily.

2 Boil the potatoes with the mint in lightly salted water until just tender. Boil the beans and broccoli in separate pans for 3–5 minutes: they should be crisp. Drain the vegetables and set aside.

3 Drain, skin and flake the cod. Shell and halve the eggs. Arrange the fish, eggs and vegetables on a large dish, garnished with the prawns.

4 To make the aioli, crush the garlic with a pinch of salt in a bowl, then whisk in the egg yolks. Whisk in the oil, a drop at a time, and season with lemon juice or vinegar, salt and pepper. Serve with the salad.

Poached Fish in a Spicy Tomato and Garlic Sauce

Serves 6

300ml/½ pint/1¼ cups passata (bottled strained tomatoes)

150ml/¼ pint/⅔ cup fish stock

1 large onion, chopped

60ml/4 tbsp chopped fresh coriander (cilantro) leaves

60ml/4 tbsp chopped fresh parsley

5–8 garlic cloves, crushed

chopped fresh chilli or chilli paste, to taste

large pinch of ground ginger

large pinch of curry powder

1.5ml/¼ tsp ground cumin

1.5ml/¼ tsp ground turmeric

seeds from 2–3 cardamom pods

juice of 2 lemons, plus extra if necessary

30ml/2 tbsp vegetable or olive oil

1.5kg/3¼ lb cod fillets

salt and ground black pepper

In this traditional dish, chunky cod steaks are cooked in a well-flavoured sauce of tomatoes, fresh herbs and garlic. Haddock or flounder would work equally well.

1 Put the passata, stock, onion, herbs, garlic, spices, lemon juice and oil in a pan and bring to the boil. Remove the pan from the heat and add the fish fillets to the hot sauce.

2 Return to the heat and allow the sauce to boil briefly again. Reduce the heat and simmer very gently for about 5 minutes, or until the fish is tender. (Test the fish with a fork. If the flesh flakes easily, then it is cooked.)

3 Taste the sauce and adjust the seasoning, adding more lemon juice if necessary. Serve hot or warm.

Roasted Monkfish with Garlic

Serves 4

1kg/2¼lb monkfish tail, skinned
1 large or 2 small heads of garlic
5ml/1 tsp fresh thyme
30ml/2 tbsp olive oil
juice of 1 lemon
2 bay leaves
salt and ground black pepper
green beans, to serve

When tied up and roasted in this way, a monkfish tail is known in French as a "gigot", because it resembles a leg of lamb. The garlic pulp can be squeezed out of the cloves at the table and spread over the fish.

1 Preheat the oven to 220°C/425°F/Gas 7. Remove any membrane from the monkfish tail and cut out the central bone. Peel 2 garlic cloves and slice thinly. Sprinkle about a quarter of these and half the thyme leaves over the cut side of the fish, then close it and tie into a neat shape using fine string. Pat dry with kitchen paper.

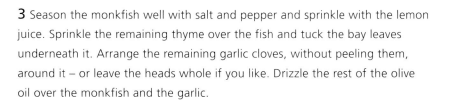

2 Make incisions along each side of the fish and insert the remaining slivers of garlic. Heat half the olive oil in a large, heavy frying pan that can be used safely in the oven, and fry the fish for about 5 minutes, turning until evenly browned all over.

3 Season the monkfish well with salt and pepper and sprinkle with the lemon juice. Sprinkle the remaining thyme over the fish and tuck the bay leaves underneath it. Arrange the remaining garlic cloves, without peeling them, around it – or leave the heads whole if you like. Drizzle the rest of the olive oil over the monkfish and the garlic.

4 Roast the monkfish for 20–25 minutes, until cooked through. Using a fish slice or metal spatula, transfer the fish and garlic to a bed of steamed green beans in a warm serving dish. Remove and discard the string, cut the fish into thick slices and serve immediately.

Whether you are using one or two cloves or several whole heads of garlic, roasting, braising or casseroling it in meat dishes brings out its creamy sweetness, enhancing the flavour of the meat and creating fragrant, enticing gravies and sauces.

Lamb Roasted with Garlic and Artichokes

Serves 6–8

1 leg of lamb, about 2kg/4½lb
1–2 heads of garlic, divided into cloves, peeled and thinly sliced, leaving 5–6 cloves peeled but whole
handful of fresh rosemary sprigs
30–60ml/2–4 tbsp olive oil
500ml/17fl oz/2¼ cups red wine
4 globe artichokes
a little lemon juice
5 shallots, chopped
250ml/8fl oz/1 cup beef stock
salt and ground black pepper

Globe artichokes are a classic feature of Roman cookery, and here they are roasted around a leg of lamb, which is generously studded with slivers of garlic and rosemary sprigs and cooked in red wine. Serve the dish accompanied by a crisp green salad with garlic croûtons.

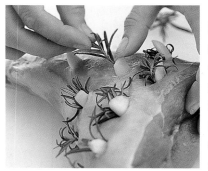

1 Make incisions all over the leg of lamb and insert a sliver of garlic and a small sprig of rosemary in each. Season with salt and plenty of pepper. Put the meat in a non-metallic dish, pour over the oil and half the wine and leave to marinate until you are ready to roast it (or cover the dish and leave in the refrigerator for up to 1 day).

2 Preheat the oven to 230°C/450°F/Gas 8. Put the meat and its juices into a roasting pan and surround with the whole garlic cloves. Roast for 10–15 minutes, then reduce the temperature to 160°C/325°F/Gas 3 and cook for 1¼ hours, or until the lamb is cooked to your liking.

Cooking to Taste

For rare lamb, cook as described. For medium, cook for 30–45 minutes more. For well done, cook for 1½ hours more. The temperatures for a meat thermometer are 60°C/140°F, 70°C/158°F, and 80°C/176°F respectively.

3 Remove the tough leaves from the artichokes, trim the bases and cut into quarters, removing the inedible choke. Drop the pieces into acidulated water as you go to stop them discolouring. Drain the artichokes and put them around the meat about 20 minutes before the end of cooking.

4 When cooked, transfer the meat and artichokes to a warmed serving dish. Spoon the fat off the pan juices and add the chopped shallots. Deglaze the pan with the remaining wine, reducing it over a high heat, then add the beef stock and cook, stirring constantly, until the shallots are soft and the sauce has thickened. Pour over the meat and serve immediately.

Lamb Casserole with Garlic and Broad Beans

Serves 6

45ml/3 tbsp olive oil

1.5kg/3–3½lb lamb fillet, cut into 5cm/2in cubes

1 large onion, chopped

6 plump garlic cloves, unpeeled

1 bay leaf

5ml/1 tsp paprika

120ml/4fl oz/½ cup dry sherry

115g/4oz shelled broad (fava) beans

30ml/2 tbsp chopped fresh parsley

salt and ground black pepper

This recipe has a Spanish influence and makes a substantial meal when served with potatoes. Garlic and sherry enrich the sauce.

1 Heat 30ml/2 tbsp of the oil in a large, flameproof casserole. Brown the meat well all over in small batches, removing each batch when done.

2 Add the remaining oil to the pan and cook the onion for about 5 minutes, until soft. Return the meat to the casserole with the garlic, bay leaf, paprika and sherry. Bring to the boil, cover and simmer gently for 1½–2 hours, until the meat is tender.

3 Add the broad beans to the dish and cook for about 10 minutes more. Stir in the parsley just before serving.

Pork with Garlic and Juniper

Serves 4

25g/1oz dried porcini mushrooms
4 pork escalopes (US pork scallops)
10ml/2 tsp balsamic vinegar
8 garlic cloves, unpeeled
15g/½oz/1 tbsp butter
45ml/3 tbsp Marsala
several fresh rosemary sprigs
10 juniper berries, crushed
salt and ground black pepper

In this quickly assembled dish, Sicilian Marsala, a fortified wine, is used to make a rich, fruity sauce enhanced by the tang of juniper and the creamy softness of cooked whole garlic cloves. Serve the pork with noodles and crisp-tender green vegetables.

1 Put the dried mushrooms in a small bowl and add enough hot water to cover. Leave to soak for 20–30 minutes, then drain, reserving the liquid.

2 Meanwhile, brush the pork all over with half the balsamic vinegar and season well with salt and pepper. Cook the garlic cloves in a small pan of boiling water for 10 minutes, until soft. Drain and set aside.

3 Melt the butter in a large, heavy frying pan. Add the pork and cook briskly until browned on both sides. Add the Marsala and rosemary, the drained mushrooms with 60ml/4 tbsp of the reserved soaking liquid, the garlic, juniper berries and remaining balsamic vinegar.

4 Simmer over a low heat for about 3 minutes, until the pork is tender and cooked through. Season the sauce to taste with salt and pepper. Transfer to warmed individual plates, spooning the Marsala sauce over the pork escalopes, and serve immediately.

Pot-roasted Garlic Brisket

Serves 6–8

5 onions, sliced

3 bay leaves

1–1.6kg/2¼–3½lb beef brisket

1 head of garlic, separated into cloves

4 carrots, thickly sliced

5–10ml/1–2 tsp paprika

500ml/17fl oz/2¼ cups beef stock

3–4 large potatoes, peeled and quartered

salt and ground black pepper

For the kishke:

250g/9oz/2¼ cups plain (all-purpose) flour

75g/3oz/½ cup semolina or couscous

15ml/1 tbsp paprika

1 carrot, grated, and 2 carrots, diced

250ml/8fl oz/1 cup rendered chicken fat

30ml/2 tbsp crisp fried onions

½ onion, grated, and 3 onions, thinly sliced

3 garlic cloves, chopped

salt and ground black pepper

90cm/36in sausage casing

In this hearty dish, pot-roasted beef is accompanied by the Jewish dumplings called kishke, traditionally made using sausage casings.

1 Preheat the oven to 180°C/350°F/Gas 4. Put one-third of the onions, with a bay leaf, in an ovenproof dish and lay the beef on top. Add the garlic, carrots and remaining bay leaves, sprinkle with salt, pepper and paprika, then top with the remaining onions. Pour in the stock, cover and roast for 2 hours.

2 Make the kishke by combining all the ingredients. Stuff the mixture into the casing and tie into sausage-shaped lengths, leaving space for expansion.

3 Add the kishke and potatoes to the pot-roast and cook for a further hour, until the meat and potatoes are tender. Raise the temperature to 200°C/400°F/Gas 6. Move the onions away from the top of the meat and return the dish, uncovered, to the oven for a further 30 minutes to brown the meat.

Corsican Beef with Macaroni

Serves 4

25g/1oz dried porcini mushrooms
6 garlic cloves
900g/2lb stewing beef, cut into
5cm/2in cubes
115g/4oz streaky (fatty) bacon, cut
into strips
45ml/3 tbsp olive oil
2 onions, sliced
300ml/½ pint/1¼ cups dry white wine
30ml/2 tbsp passata (bottled
strained tomatoes)
pinch of ground cinnamon
fresh rosemary sprig
1 bay leaf
225g/8oz/2 cups large macaroni
50g/2oz/⅔ cup freshly grated
Parmesan cheese
salt and ground black pepper

In Corsica, pasta is often dressed with gravy and served as an accompaniment to meat dishes. Here, it takes up the rich garlic flavour of this beef stew.

1 Soak the dried mushrooms in hot water for 20–30 minutes, then drain, reserving the liquid. Cut three of the garlic cloves into slivers. Make small incisions in the pieces of beef and push pieces of garlic and bacon into them. Season the meat with salt and pepper.

2 Heat the oil in a heavy pan. Brown the meat well on all sides, adding it to the pan in small batches and transferring the pieces to a plate as they are done. Add the sliced onions to the pan and cook until lightly browned. Crush the remaining garlic and add it to the pan, with the meat.

3 Stir in the wine, passata, mushrooms, cinnamon, rosemary and bay leaf, and season with salt and pepper. Cook gently for 30 minutes, stirring often. Add the mushroom liquid and enough water to cover the meat. Bring to the boil and simmer gently, covered, for 3 hours, until the meat is very tender.

4 Cook the macaroni in a large pan of lightly salted, boiling water for about 10 minutes, or until *al dente*. Lift the meat out of the gravy and transfer to a serving dish. Drain the pasta and layer it in a serving dish with the gravy and grated cheese. Serve with the meat.

Chicken Cooked in Port with Forty Cloves of Garlic

Serves 4–5

6 heads of garlic
15g/½oz/1 tbsp butter
45ml/3 tbsp olive oil
1.8–2kg/4–4½lb chicken
5ml/1 tsp plain (all-purpose) flour
75ml/5 tbsp white port
2–3 fresh tarragon or rosemary sprigs
30ml/2 tbsp crème fraîche (optional)
salt and ground black pepper

This classic French dish makes the most of garlic's magical transformation during slow, gentle cooking – from biting pungency to sweet, mellow creaminess. The whole effect is both subtle and delicious.

1 Separate three of the heads of garlic into cloves and peel them. Remove the papery outer skin from the remaining three heads. Preheat the oven to 180°C/350°F/Gas 4.

2 Heat the butter and 15ml/1 tbsp of the oil in a flameproof casserole into which the chicken and garlic will fit snugly. Brown the chicken over a medium heat, turning frequently, for 10–15 minutes.

3 Add the flour and cook, stirring, for 1 minute, then add the port. Tuck in the garlic heads and cloves, and the herbs. Pour over the remaining oil and season with salt and pepper. Cover tightly and cook in the oven for 1½ hours until cooked through.

4 Transfer the chicken and whole garlic heads to a warmed serving dish and discard the herbs. Whisk the garlic cloves into the juices. Add crème fraîche, if you like, and serve the garlic purée with the chicken.

Chicken Baked with Shallots, Garlic and Fennel

Serves 4

8 chicken portions
250g/9oz shallots, peeled
1 head of garlic, separated into cloves and peeled
60ml/4 tbsp olive oil
45ml/3 tbsp tarragon vinegar
45ml/3 tbsp white wine or vermouth
5ml/1 tsp fennel seeds, crushed
2 fennel bulbs, cut into wedges, feathery tops reserved
150ml/¼ pint/⅔ cup double (heavy) cream
5ml/1 tsp redcurrant jelly
15ml/1 tbsp tarragon mustard
30ml/2 tbsp chopped fresh parsley
salt and ground black pepper

This is a very simple and delicious way to cook chicken. If you're in a hurry, you could cut down the marinating time, but it does impart a wonderfully subtle flavour to the dish.

1 Place the chicken, shallots and garlic, reserving one clove, in an ovenproof dish. Add the oil, vinegar, wine or vermouth and fennel seeds. Season with pepper and leave in the refrigerator to marinate for 2–3 hours.

2 Preheat the oven to 190°C/375°F/Gas 5. Add the fennel to the chicken and season with salt. Bake for 50–60 minutes, stirring the dish once or twice, until the chicken juices run clear when the thickest part is pierced with a skewer or the point of a sharp knife.

3 Transfer the chicken and vegetables to a serving dish and keep warm.

4 Skim the fat off the juices in the dish and transfer the contents to a small pan, if necessary. Bring to the boil and stir in the cream, redcurrant jelly and mustard. Chop the reserved garlic clove and fennel tops. Serve the chicken with the sauce poured over, sprinkled with the garlic, fennel and parsley.

VEGETARIAN DISHES

While garlic beautifully enhances the flavours of meat and fish, it is also able to take on a starring role in vegetarian dishes, turning the simplest ingredients into gourmet treats, whether tarts, soufflés, roasted medleys or pasta.

Pasta with Garlic and Chilli

Serves 3–4

400g/14oz dried spaghetti
105ml/7 tbsp extra virgin olive oil
1.5ml/¼ tsp dried red chilli flakes
6 large garlic cloves, finely chopped
15ml/1 tbsp chopped fresh mint
15ml/1 tbsp chopped fresh parsley
salt and ground black pepper

This is the simplest of pasta dishes and, undoubtedly, one of the best. Serve it just as it is – without grated Parmesan cheese – to focus on the clear flavours of the garlic and olive oil.

1 Cook the spaghetti in a large pan of lightly salted, boiling water for about 8 minutes, or until *al dente*. Meanwhile, warm the olive oil gently in another large pan. Add the chilli flakes and cook over a very low heat, stirring occasionally, for 2–3 minutes.

2 Add the garlic to the pan and cook, stirring occasionally, for 2 minutes, without allowing it to brown. Remove the pan from the heat and add the chopped mint.

3 Drain the pasta and tip it into the oil and garlic mixture. Add the parsley, season to taste with black pepper and toss thoroughly. Turn into a warm bowl and serve immediately, offering more olive oil at the table, if you like.

Mushroom Garlic Stroganoff

Serves 6

500g/1¼lb button (white) mushrooms
50g/2oz/¼ cup butter
250g/9oz assorted wild mushrooms, cut into bitesize pieces
6 garlic cloves, chopped
2 onions, chopped
30ml/2 tbsp plain (all-purpose) flour
120ml/4fl oz/½ cup dry white wine
250ml/8fl oz/1 cup vegetable stock
250g/9oz crème fraîche
large pinch of freshly grated nutmeg
15ml/1 tbsp lemon juice
salt and ground black pepper
fresh parsley or chives, to garnish

With an interesting assortment of cultivated and wild mushrooms, this creamy dish makes a good vegetarian choice for a special meal. Serve it with a mixture of wild rices.

1 If the button mushrooms are large, cut them into halves or quarters. Melt half the butter in a pan and quickly brown all the mushrooms, in batches, over a high heat, transferring each batch to a plate when it is done. Sprinkle the mushrooms with a little of the garlic as they are cooking.

2 Add the remaining butter to the pan and cook the onions over a low heat, stirring, for about 5 minutes, until softened. Add the remaining garlic and cook for a further 1–2 minutes. Sprinkle over the flour and stir into the butter.

3 Remove the pan from the heat and gradually stir in the wine and stock. Return the pan to a low heat and bring to the boil, stirring constantly, until the sauce is thick and smooth. Add the mushrooms with their juices and the crème fraîche. Season with nutmeg, lemon juice and salt and pepper to taste. Serve hot, garnished with chopped parsley or chives.

Roasted Garlic and Aubergine Bakes with Red Pepper Dressing

Serves 6

2 large heads of garlic

6–7 fresh thyme sprigs

60ml/4 tbsp olive oil, plus extra for greasing

350g/12oz aubergines (eggplant), cut into 1cm/$\frac{1}{2}$in cubes

2 red (bell) peppers, halved and seeded

pinch of saffron threads

300ml/$\frac{1}{2}$ pint/1$\frac{1}{4}$ cups whipping cream

2 large (US extra large) eggs

pinch of sugar

30ml/2 tbsp shredded fresh basil leaves

salt and ground black pepper

For the dressing:

90ml/6 tbsp olive oil

15–25ml/1–1$\frac{1}{2}$ tbsp balsamic vinegar

115g/4oz tomatoes, peeled, seeded and finely diced

$\frac{1}{2}$ small red onion, finely chopped

generous pinch of ground roasted cumin

handful of fresh basil leaves

These little tasty aubergine and garlic treats, baked in a mould, make an elegant main course, accompanied by good bread and steamed broccoli.

1 Preheat the oven to 190°C/375°F/Gas 5. Place the garlic on a piece of foil with the thyme and sprinkle with 15ml/1 tbsp of the oil. Wrap the foil around the garlic and cook for 35–45 minutes, until soft. Reduce the oven temperature to 180°C/350°F/Gas 4.

2 Heat the remaining olive oil in a heavy pan and cook the aubergines, stirring constantly, for 5–8 minutes, until browned and cooked. Grill (broil) the peppers under a high heat, skin side up, until blackened and charred. Cover with a dishtowel and leave for 10 minutes, then peel and dice. Soak the saffron in 15ml/1 tbsp hot water for 10 minutes.

3 Unwrap the garlic and pop the cloves out of their skins into a food processor or blender. Add the oil from cooking, the cream and eggs and process until smooth. Add the saffron and its liquid and season with salt, pepper and sugar. Stir in half the diced pepper and the basil.

4 Oil six large ovenproof ramekins and line the base of each with baking parchment. Divide the aubergines among the dishes and add the egg mixture. Cover each dish with foil and pierce a hole for steam to escape. Stand them in a roasting pan and add hot water to come halfway up the sides. Bake for 25–30 minutes, until just set.

Using a bain-marie

The roasting pan of hot water that the pot stands in, sometimes called a bain-marie, helps the bakes to cook evenly without burning. Top up the water, if necessary.

5 Make the dressing while the bakes are cooking. Whisk the oil and vinegar with salt and pepper. Stir in the tomatoes, red onion, remaining red pepper and cumin. Reserve a few basil leaves for the garnish, then chop the rest and add to the dressing.

6 Leave the bakes to cool for about 5 minutes before turning them out on to warmed serving plates and surrounding with the dressing. Garnish with fresh basil leaves and serve.

Roasted Garlic and Goat's Cheese Soufflés

Serves 4

2 large, plump heads of garlic
3 fresh thyme sprigs
15ml/1 tbsp olive oil
250ml/8fl oz/1 cup milk
1 bay leaf
2 × 1cm/½ in thick onion slices
2 cloves
50g/2oz/¼ cup butter
40g/1½ oz/⅓ cup plain (all-purpose)
flour, sifted
3 eggs, separated, plus 1 egg white
150g/5oz goat's cheese, crumbled
50g/2oz/⅔ cup freshly grated
Parmesan cheese
5ml/1 tsp chopped fresh thyme
2.5ml/½ tsp cream of tartar
salt, ground black pepper
and cayenne pepper

The mellow flavour of roasted garlic pervades these simple soufflés. The ideal accompaniment is a salad of peppery leaves.

1 Preheat the oven to 190°C/375°F/Gas 5. Wrap the garlic in foil with the thyme and oil and bake for 35–45 minutes, until soft. When cool, squeeze the garlic pulp out of the skins and purée with the cooking oil.

2 Meanwhile, place the milk, bay leaf, onion slices and cloves in a pan and bring to the boil. Remove from the heat and leave to infuse (steep) for 30 minutes. Preheat the oven to 200°C/400°F/Gas 6.

3 Melt 40g/1½ oz/3 tbsp of the butter in another pan. Stir in the flour and cook gently, stirring, for 2 minutes. Reheat and strain the milk, then gradually stir it into the flour and butter. Cook gently for 10 minutes, stirring constantly. Season with salt, pepper and cayenne and cool slightly.

4 Beat in the egg yolks, one at a time, then beat in the goat's cheese, Parmesan, reserving 15ml/1 tbsp, and the thyme. Use the remaining butter to grease four large ramekins (about 250ml/8fl oz/1 cup).

5 Whisk the egg whites with the cream of tartar until firm but not dry. Stir 45ml/3 tbsp of the whites into the sauce, then gently fold in the remainder. Pour the mixture into the dishes and sprinkle with the reserved Parmesan.

6 Cook the soufflés on a baking sheet for about 20 minutes. They should be risen and firm to a light touch in the centre. Serve immediately.

Shallot and Garlic Tarte Tatin

Serves 4–6

300g/11oz puff pastry
50g/2oz/¼ cup butter
75g/3oz/1 cup freshly grated Parmesan
cheese
flour, for dusting

For the topping:
40g/1½oz/3 tbsp butter
500g/1¼lb shallots
12–16 large garlic cloves, peeled
15ml/1 tbsp golden caster
(superfine) sugar
15ml/1 tbsp balsamic or sherry vinegar
45ml/3 tbsp water
5ml/1 tsp chopped fresh thyme
salt and ground black pepper

In this savoury version of the classic apple tarte Tatin, caramelized garlic cloves and shallots are cooked under a layer of crisp Parmesan pastry. It's a delicious accompaniment to a salad of mixed leaves, pears and cheese.

1 Roll out the pastry on a lightly floured surface into a rectangle and spread the butter over the top two-thirds, to within 2.5cm/1in of the edge. Sprinkle the grated Parmesan over the butter. Fold the bottom third up and the top third down. Seal the edges, roll out again and fold as before. Wrap and chill for 30 minutes.

2 To make the topping, melt the butter in a 23–25cm/9–10in frying pan that will safely go in the oven. Add the shallots and garlic and cook over a low heat, stirring occasionally, until lightly browned.

3 Add the sugar and increase the heat. Cook until the sugar begins to caramelize, turning the shallots and garlic in the butter. Add the vinegar, water, thyme and seasoning. Part cover and cook for 5–8 minutes.

4 Preheat the oven to 190°C/375°F/ Gas 5. Roll out the pastry to fit the pan and lay it over the shallots and garlic. Prick the surface and bake for 25–35 minutes, or until the pastry is golden. Leave to rest for 5–10 minutes, then invert on to a serving dish.

SIDE DISHES

When you are serving plainly roasted or grilled meat or fish, use garlic to add extra flavour and interest to vegetable accompaniments. The earthy flavours of root vegetables and lentils are wonderfully enlivened by the addition of garlic and spices.

Potatoes Baked with Fennel, Onions, Garlic and Saffron

Serves 4–6

500g/1¼lb small waxy potatoes, cut into wedges
12–15 saffron threads
1 head of garlic, separated into cloves
12 small red or yellow onions, peeled
3 fennel bulbs, cut into wedges, feathery tops reserved
4–6 bay leaves
6–9 fresh thyme sprigs
175ml/6fl oz/¾ cup fish, chicken or vegetable stock
30ml/2 tbsp sherry vinegar
2.5ml/½ tsp sugar
5ml/1 tsp fennel seeds, lightly crushed
2.5ml/½ tsp paprika
45ml/3 tbsp olive oil
salt and ground black pepper

Serve this subtly flavoured and attractive mixture with fish or chicken, or to accompany an egg-based main course dish.

1 Boil the potatoes in salted water for 8–10 minutes. Drain. Preheat the oven to 190°C/375°F/Gas 5. Place the saffron in a small bowl, add 30ml/2 tbsp warm water and leave to soak for 10 minutes.

2 Peel and chop 2 garlic cloves. Place the potatoes, onions, unpeeled garlic, fennel wedges, bay leaves and thyme in an ovenproof dish. Combine the stock, saffron and soaking liquid, vinegar and sugar, and pour over the vegetables. Add the fennel seeds, paprika, garlic and oil, and season.

3 Bake for 1–1¼ hours, stirring occasionally, until tender. Chop the fennel leaves, sprinkle over and serve.

Garlic Mashed Potatoes

The sweet flavour of cooked garlic is readily absorbed by these creamy mashed potatoes, which are delicious with all kinds of roast and grilled meats, as well as vegetarian dishes.

1 Preheat the oven to 200°C/400°F/Gas 6. Bring a small pan of water to the boil, add two-thirds of the garlic cloves, bring back to the boil and cook for 2 minutes. Drain and peel the cloves. Place the remaining garlic cloves in a roasting pan and bake for 30–40 minutes.

2 Melt half the butter in a heavy frying pan and cook the blanched garlic cloves, covered, for 20–25 minutes, until tender and just golden. Remove the pan from the heat and cool, then process the contents to a smooth paste in a food processor or blender.

3 Cook the potatoes in salted, boiling water until tender, then drain and mash. Return to the pan over a medium heat and stir for 1–2 minutes to dry out completely.

4 Heat the milk and gradually beat it into the potatoes with the remaining butter and garlic purée. Season with salt and pepper and serve with the roasted garlic cloves.

Serves 6–8

3 heads of garlic, separated into cloves, unpeeled
115g/4oz/½ cup unsalted (sweet) butter
1.5kg/3lb baking potatoes, quartered
120–175ml/4–6fl oz/½–¾ cup milk
salt and ground black pepper

Cauliflower with Garlic Crumbs

Serves 4–6

1 large cauliflower, cut into
bitesize florets
90–120ml/6–8 tbsp olive oil
130g/4½oz/2¼ cups dry white or
wholemeal (whole-wheat) breadcrumbs
3–5 garlic cloves, chopped
salt and ground black pepper

*Garlic breadcrumbs add both texture and flavour to this dish. Serve it as
an accompaniment to meat or fish, or sprinkled on to a pasta sauce.*

1 Steam or boil the cauliflower in lightly salted water until just tender. Drain
well and leave to cool.

2 Heat 60–75ml/4–5 tbsp of the oil in a pan, add the breadcrumbs and toss
over a medium heat until browned and crisp. Add the garlic, turn once or
twice, then remove from the pan and set aside.

3 Add the remaining oil to the pan and lightly brown the cauliflower in it.
Stir in the garlic crumbs, season with salt and pepper and serve hot or warm.

Red Onion and Garlic Relish

Serves 6

45ml/3 tbsp olive oil
3 large red onions, sliced
2 heads of garlic, separated into cloves
and peeled
10ml/2 tsp coriander seeds, crushed
10ml/2 tsp light muscovado (brown)
sugar, plus a little extra, if necessary
pinch of saffron threads, soaked in
45ml/3 tbsp warm water
5cm/2in cinnamon stick
2 bay leaves
30ml/2 tbsp sherry vinegar
juice of ½ small orange
30ml/2 tbsp chopped preserved lemon
salt and ground black pepper

This powerful relish is flavoured with North African spices and preserved lemons, and is delicious with grilled lamb or chicken. It tastes best if made in advance and left to stand for 24 hours.

1 Heat the oil in a heavy pan, stir in the onions, then cover and reduce the heat. Cook for 10–15 minutes, stirring occasionally, until the onions are soft. Add the garlic and coriander seeds, cover and cook for a further 5–8 minutes.

2 Add the sugar and salt and pepper and cook, uncovered, for 5 minutes. Add the saffron with its soaking water, the cinnamon stick and bay leaves. Stir in the vinegar and orange juice.

3 Cook gently, uncovered, until the onions are very soft and most of the liquid has evaporated. Stir in the preserved lemon and cook for 5 minutes. Adjust the seasoning, adding more sugar if necessary. Serve warm or cool.

Jerusalem Artichokes with Garlic, Shallots and Bacon

Serves 4

50g/2oz/¼ cup butter
115g/4oz smoked bacon or pancetta, diced
800g/1¾lb Jerusalem artichokes, peeled
8–12 garlic cloves, peeled
115g/4oz shallots, chopped
75ml/5 tbsp water
30ml/2 tbsp olive oil
25g/1oz/½ cup fresh white breadcrumbs
30–45ml/2–3 tbsp chopped fresh parsley
salt and ground black pepper

The smoky, earthy flavour of Jerusalem artichokes is a wonderful foil for garlic, and this dish goes well with chicken, roast cod or monkfish, and with pork. Drop the artichokes into acidulated water as you peel them, to prevent them from discolouring.

1 Melt half the butter in a heavy pan, add the bacon or pancetta and cook over a medium heat, stirring occasionally, until just beginning to crisp. Using a slotted spoon, remove half of it and set aside.

2 Add the Jerusalem artichokes, garlic and shallots and cook, stirring frequently, for about 5–8 minutes, until slightly browned. Season to taste with salt and pepper and stir in the water. Lower the heat, cover and cook gently for 8–10 minutes.

3 Uncover the pan, increase the heat and cook for 5–6 minutes until the artichokes are tender and the liquid has completely evaporated.

4 In another pan, melt the remaining butter with the oil, and cook the breadcrumbs, stirring, until crisp and golden. Add the chopped parsley and the reserved bacon or pancetta. Stir the mixture through the artichokes and serve immediately.